BOOK of DAYS

Book of Days

Artwork copyright © 1998 Royal Doulton
Royal Doulton is a trademark. Used under licence by Garborg's, Inc.
Design by Garborg Design Works
Text copyright © 1998 by Garborg's, Inc.
Published by Garborg's, Inc.
P.O. Box 20132, Bloomington, MN 55420

All rights reserved. No part of this book may be reproduced in any form without permission in writing from the publisher.

Scripture quotations marked NIV are taken from the HOLY BIBLE, NEW INTERNATIONAL VERSION®. Copyright © 1973, 1978, 1984 by International Bible Society. All rights reserved.

Scripture quotations marked TLB are taken from The Living Bible, © 1971. Used by permission of Tyndale House Publishers, Inc., Wheaton, IL 60189. All rights reserved.

ISBN 1-58375-415-6

A place to record
birthdays, anniversaries,
and other special occasions.

Today a new sun rises for me;
everything lives,
everything is animated,
everything seems to speak to
me of my passion,
everything invites me to cherish it.

ANNE DE LENCLOS

January

1

2

3

4

*Reach high,
for stars lie hidden
in your soul.
Dream deep,
for every
dream precedes
the goal.*

Pamela Vaull Starr

January

5

6

7

8

January

9

10

11

12

JANUARY

13

The innocent brightness of new born day is lovely yet.

WILLIAM
WORDSWORTH

14

15

16

JANUARY

17

18

19

A thing of beauty is a joy forever: Its loveliness increases; it will never Pass into nothingness.

20

JOHN KEATS

JANUARY

21

22

23

24

January

25

26

27

28

JANUARY

It's the little things that make up the richest part of the tapestry of our lives.

29

30

31

*Love knows no limit to its endurance,
no end to its trust,
no fading of its hope;
it can outlast anything.
Love never fails.*

1 CORINTHIANS 13:7-8 PHILLIPS

February

1

2

Heard melodies are sweet, but those unheard Are sweeter.

JOHN KEATS

3

4

FEBRUARY

5

6

7

8

February

9

10

11

12

FEBRUARY

13

14

> The best and most beautiful things in the world cannot be seen or even touched. They must be felt with the heart.
>
> HELEN KELLER

15

16

February

17

18

19

20

Beauty is simply reality seen with the eyes of love.

Evelyn Underhill

February

21

22

23

24

February

25

26

27

28

February

29

All the things in this world are gifts and signs of God's love to us. The whole world is a love letter from God.

Peter Kreeft

There is joy that will not cease,
Calm hovering o'er the face of things,
That sweet tranquillity and peace
That morning ever brings.

JOHN CLARE

March

1

2

3

Friendship gives a voice to the heart and wings to the soul.

4

March

5

6

7

8

March

9

10

11

12

MARCH

Kind words are jewels that live in the heart and soul and remain as blessed memories years after they have been spoken.

MARVEA JOHNSON

13

14

15

16

March

17

18

19

20

Do not linger to gather flowers to keep them, but walk on, for flowers will keep themselves blooming all your way.

RABINDRANATH TAGORE

March

21

22

23

24

March

25

26

27

28

March

29

30

See! The winter is past; the rains are over and gone. Flowers appear on the earth; the season of singing has come.

31

Song of Songs 2:11-12 niv

Cherish your visions, cherish your ideals,
the beauty that forms in your mind, the
for out of them will grow all delightful

Cherish the music that stirs in your heart, loveliness that drapes your purest thoughts, conditions, all heavenly environment.

— JAMES ALLEN

The heart of a friend is a wondrous thing,
A gift of God most fair;
For the seed of friendship there sprouts and grows
to love and beauty rare....
May I carefully tend the seed which grows
In friendship's garden there.

PAT LASSEN

April

April

1

2

3

4

The beauty of the earth, the beauty of the sky, the order of the stars, the sun, the moon...their very loveliness is their confession of God.

AUGUSTINE

April

5

6

7

8

April

9

10

11

12

APRIL

13

Our Lord has written the promise of the resurrection, not in books alone, but in every leaf in springtime.

MARTIN LUTHER

14

15

16

April

17

18

19

To be able to find joy in another's joy, that is the secret of happiness.

20

GEORGE BERNANOS

April

21

22

23

24

April

25

26

27

28

APRIL

Friendship is a sheltering tree; Oh, the joys that come down shower-like!

SAMUEL TAYLOR COLERIDGE

29

30

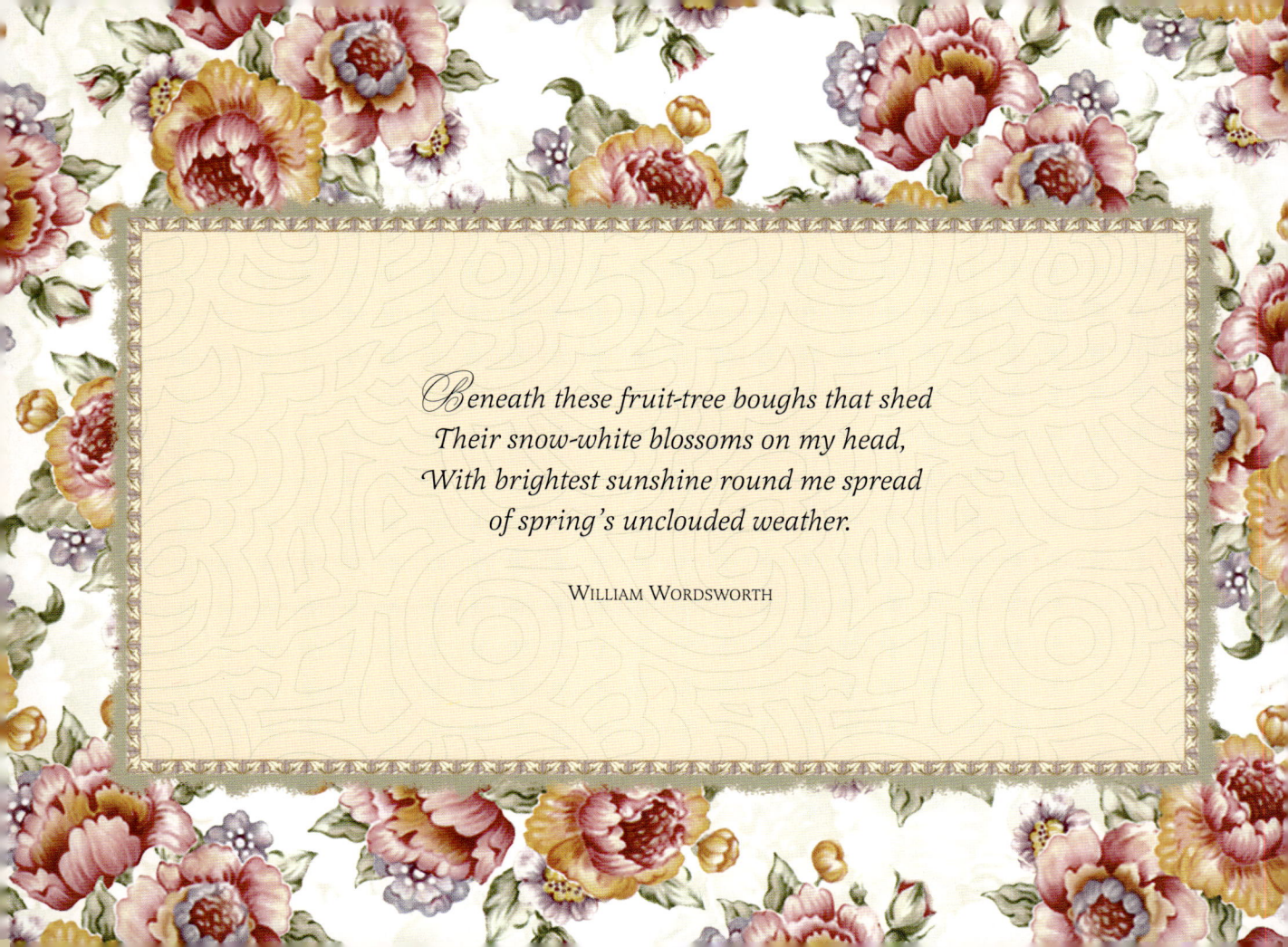

*Beneath these fruit-tree boughs that shed
Their snow-white blossoms on my head,
With brightest sunshine round me spread
of spring's unclouded weather.*

WILLIAM WORDSWORTH

May

1

2

> *Friendship is the breathing rose, with sweets in every fold.*
>
> OLIVER WENDELL HOLMES

3

4

May

5

6

7

8

May

9

10

11

12

MAY

13

14

Kind words can be short and easy to speak, but their echoes are truly endless.

MOTHER TERESA

15

16

May

17

18

19

20

It is God...who made the garden grow in your hearts.

1 Corinthians 3:6 TLB

May

21

22

23

24

May

25

26

27

28

MAY

29

30

What the dew is to the flower, gentle words are to the soul.

POLLY RUPE

31

His tenderness in the springing grass,
His beauty in the flowers,
His living love in the sun above—
All here, and near, and ours.

CHARLOTTE PERKINS GILMAN

June

1

2

3

Being with you is like walking on a very clear morning— definitely the sensation of belonging there.

E. B. White

4

JUNE

5

6

7

8

June

9

10

11

12

JUNE

May your roots go down deep into the soil of God's marvelous love.

Ephesians 3:17 TLB

13

14

15

16

June

17

18

> *"Just living is not enough," said the butterfly. "One must have sunshine, freedom, and a little flower."*
>
> HANS CHRISTIAN ANDERSEN

19

20

June

21

22

23

24

June

25

26

27

28

June

29

30

How wonderful it is that nobody need wait a single moment before starting to improve the world.

ANNE FRANK

*I have a garden of my own,
Shining with flowers of every hue;
I loved it dearly while alone,
But I shall love it more with you.*

THOMAS MOORE

July

1

2

3

4

> *If I had a single flower for every time I think about you, I could walk forever in my garden.*
>
> Claudia A. Grandí

July

5

6

7

8

July

9

10

11

12

JULY

13

Like the summer breezes playing, like the tall trees softly swaying… is the perfect peace of God.

MICHAEL PERRY

14

15

16

July

17

18

19

20

There is beauty in the sunlight and the soft blue beams above. Oh, the world is full of beauty when the heart is full of love.

July

21

22

23

24

July

25

26

27

28

July

Peace within makes beauty without.

ENGLISH PROVERB

29

30

31

"Hope" is the thing with feathers
That perches in the soul—
And sings the tune without the words
And never stops—at all.

EMILY DICKINSON

August

1

2

3

4

How beautiful a day can be when kindness touches it

— George Elliston

August

5

6

7

8

August

9

10

11

12

AUGUST

13

14

15

He has made everything beautiful in its time.

ECCLESIASTES 3:11 NIV

16

August

17

18

19

20

The sun does not shine for a few trees and flowers, but for the wide world's joy.

Henery Ward Beecher

August

21

22

23

24

August

25

26

27

28

August

29

30

Gather buds of friendship; keep them till full-blown; You will find more happiness than you have ever known.

Amy R. Raabe

31

The happiness of life is made the little soon~forgotten charities a heartfelt compliment.

...up of minute fractions...
of a kiss or smile, a kind look,

SAMUEL TAYLOR COLERIDGE

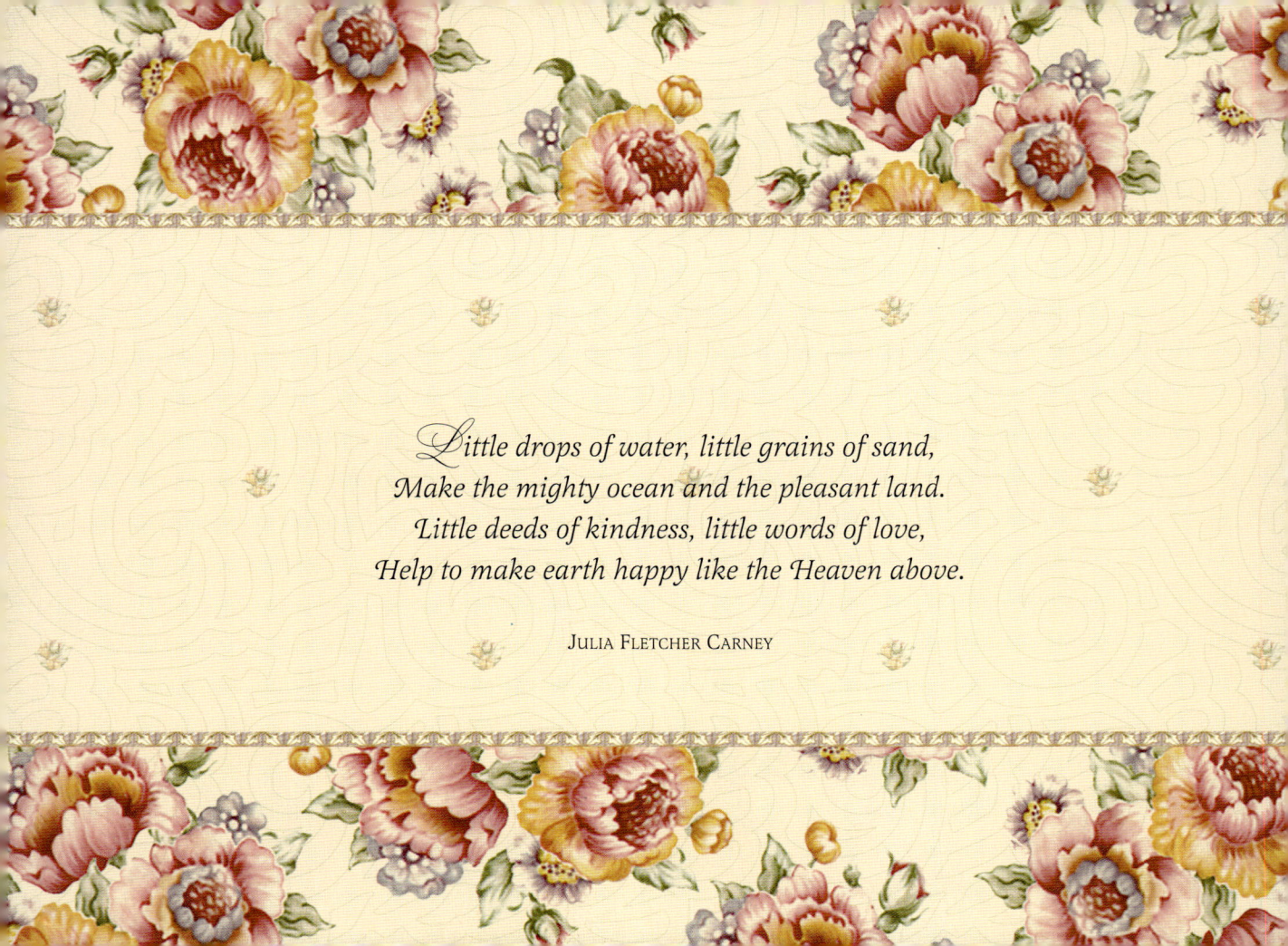

Little drops of water, little grains of sand,
Make the mighty ocean and the pleasant land.
Little deeds of kindness, little words of love,
Help to make earth happy like the Heaven above.

JULIA FLETCHER CARNEY

September

1

2

3

4

There are no days in life so memorable as those which vibrated to some stroke of the imagination.

Ralph Waldo Emerson

September

5

6

7

8

September

9

10

11

12

September

When you least expect it, a common thread...begins to weave together the fabric of friendship.

MARY KAY SHANLEY

13

14

15

16

September

17

18

The moments of happiness we enjoy take us by surprise. It is not that we seize them, but that they seize us.

ASHLEY MONTAGU

19

20

September

21

22

23

24

September

25

26

27

28

September

_____ 29

_____ 30

What lies behind us, and what lies before us are tiny matters, compared to what lies within us.

RALPH WALDO EMERSON

Hold fast your dreams!
Within your heart
Keep one still, secret spot
Where dreams may go
And, sheltered so,
May thrive and grow.

Louise Driscoll

October

October

1

2

3

4

Looking forward to things is half the pleasure of them.

LUCY MAUD MONTGOMERY

October

5

6

7

8

OCTOBER

9

10

11

12

October

13

I am beginning to learn that it is the sweet, simple things of life which are the real ones after all.

14

LAURA INGALLS WILDER

15

16

OCTOBER

17

18

19

20

Happy times and bygone days are never lost.... In truth, they grow more wonderful within the heart that keeps them.

KAY ANDREW

October

21

22

23

24

October

25

26

27

28

OCTOBER

Seeds of kindness will yield a bountiful harvest of blessings.

29

30

31

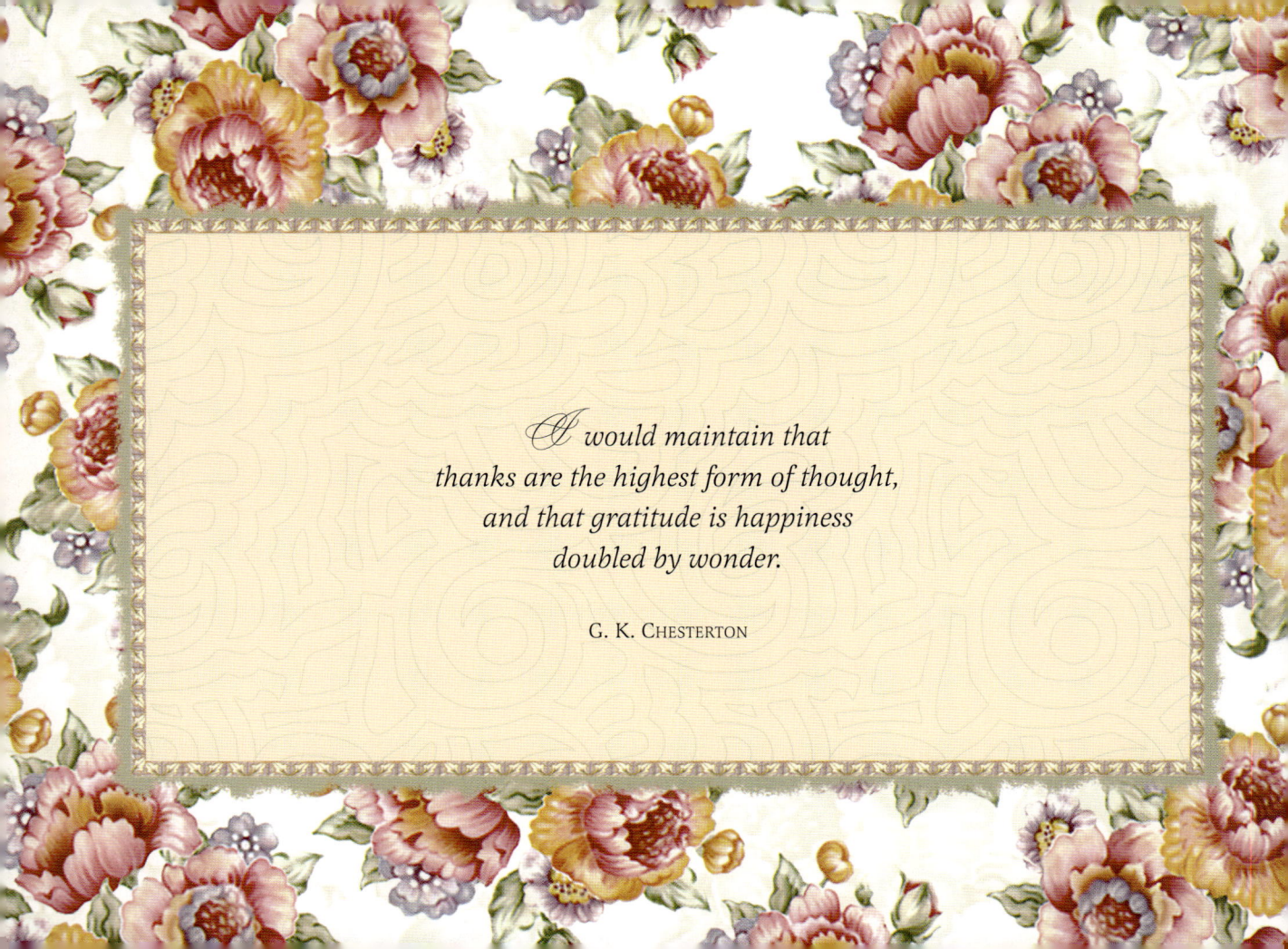

*I would maintain that
thanks are the highest form of thought,
and that gratitude is happiness
doubled by wonder.*

G. K. Chesterton

November

1

2

Take time to give thanks for the beauty of today.

3

4

November

5

6

7

8

November

9

10

11

12

November

13

14

Your greatest pleasure is that which rebounds from hearts that you have made glad.

15

HENRY WARD BEECHER

16

November

17

18

19

20

Give thanks to the Lord, for he is good; his love endures forever.

1 Chronicles 16:34 NIV

November

21

22

23

24

November

25

26

27

28

November

29

30

There is something in every season, in every day, to celebrate with thanksgiving.

GLORIA GAITHER

*Many merry Christmases,
many happy New Years.
Unbroken friendships,
great accumulations of cheerful recollections
and affections on earth, and heaven for us all.*

CHARLES DICKENS

December

1

2

3

It is a fine seasoning for joy to think of those we love.

4

Molière

December

5

6

7

8

December

9

10

11

12

December

*Love came down at Christmas,
Love all lovely, love divine;
Love was born at Christmas,
Star and angels gave the sign.*

CHRISTINA ROSSETTI

13

14

15

16

December

17

18

> *Behold, a virgin shall be with child, and shall bring forth a son, and they shall call his name Emmanuel... God with us.*
>
> MATTHEW 1:23 KJV

19

20

December

21

22

23

24

December

25

26

27

28

December

29

30

31

Every gift of kindness bears the signature of love.

Janet L. Weaver